WHAT IS CHRIST- -IANITY?

FAITH & MORALITY RECONSIDERED

Scripture quotations are translated directly from the original German presentation.

Published by:
1517 Publishing
PO Box 54032
Irvine, CA 92619-4032

Publisher's Cataloging-In-Publication Data
(Prepared by Cassidy Cataloguing Services)

Names: Pieper, Franz, 1852-1931, author. | Bartelt, Philip, translator.
Title: What is Christianity? : faith & morality reconsidered / presentation by
    Francis Pieper ; delivered in German & translated by Pastor Philip Bartelt.
Other titles: What is Christ-ianity? | Wesen des Christentums. English
Description: Irvine, CA : 1517 Publishing, [2023] | Includes bibliographical
    references.
Identifiers: ISBN: 978-1-956658-30-9 (paperback) | 978-1-956658-31-6 (ebook)
Subjects: LCSH: Christianity. | Theology. | Christian life. | Lutheran Church. |
    LCGFT: Lectures. | BISAC: RELIGION / Christianity / Lutheran. | RELIGION /
    Christianity / General. | RELIGION / Christian Theology / General.
Classification: LCC: BX8066.P555 D3713 2023 | DDC: 252.041—dc23

Printed in the United States of America.

Cover art by Zachariah James Stuef.

WHAT IS CHRIST- -IANITY?

FAITH & MORALITY RECONSIDERED

PRESENTATION BY
FRANCIS PIEPER

DELIVERED IN GERMAN & TRANSLATED BY
PASTOR PHILIP BARTELT

FIFTEEN·SEVENTEEN PUBLISHING

1517.

Francis Pieper: An Historical and Theological Sketch

Born Franz August Otto Pieper on June 27, 1852, in Carwitz, Pomerania, Francis Pieper would become and remain one of the most influential theologians for American Lutheranism in the 20th century. As a young boy he was educated at the German Gymnasium in Koeslin, but around his eighteenth birthday in 1870, he, his mother, and three younger brothers would emigrate to the United States to join Francis's two older brothers who already were living in Wisconsin. Of these, his older brother Reinhold would go on to become a professor of homiletics and president of Concordia Theological Seminary for the Lutheran Church—Missouri Synod (LCMS), while his younger brother August would go on to be a seminary professor for the Wisconsin Evangelical Lutheran Synod (WELS). While in the U.S., Pieper would continue his education at Northwestern College in Watertown, WI. He graduated in 1872 and was selected to deliver the commencement speech, which he delivered in Latin, about what it meant to be German and Lutheran in America. He then moved to Concordia Seminary, St. Louis, where he studied, notably, under C. F. W. Walther, to whom he would later become a successor both in his theology and his leadership of the LCMS. Pieper graduated in 1875 and was called and ordained in Centerville, WI. During his short time of pastoring, Pieper met his bride-to-be, Minnie Koehn, whom he married on January 2, 1877. Shortly thereafter, in 1878 he was called from pastoral ministry into the academic scene to serve as a professor at Concordia Seminary, St. Louis, at the age of twenty-six. After over twenty years as a seminary professor, Pieper was elected as Synod President, in which position he served from 1899-1911. Throughout this time, he was a prolific writer of many essays and articles, but his greatest and most enduring work is undeniably *Christian Dogmatics*, a three-volume dogmatics which he wrote for the 400th anniversary of the Reformation. As a testament to its greatness, Pieper's dogmatics has been the standard dogmatics in the LCMS for over a century and can still be found on every LCMS pastor's shelves. Despite gestures at a new dogmatics, none has replaced Pieper as the universal standard. After a long and distinguished career as a pastor, professor, and president, Pieper died in June of 1931.

Pieper's career is remarkable for a number of reasons, one of which is that he served during a time of great transition. When Pieper became a professor in 1878, the LCMS's membership was around 150,000; by the time of his death, the membership of the LCMS had grown to over 1,000,000. With such explosive growth came explosive changes, one of the most significant of which was the transition from German to English as the standard language of Synod. The LCMS saw its first English Small Catechism and hymnal during Pieper's lifetime and under his influence. Throughout his life and by his teaching and example, Pieper formed a bridge between Germany and America in both theology and culture. With a foot in both worlds, one of Pieper's greatest theological contributions was to consider the question of Lutheran identity, which was in flux globally, but most especially for Lutherans starting anew in America.

For Pieper, to be Lutheran meant to believe in Jesus Christ as the perfect sacrifice for sins in our stead—that Jesus was put under the law, under our sin, and under our punishment, in our stead and on our behalf, so that by faith we may enjoy perfect freedom, righteousness, and salvation. It is to hold fast by faith alone to the grace of God and thereby to be justified in God's sight without works of the law. And this is not only what makes a Lutheran, but what makes a Christian and, by extension, the Christian church. The church is that group of believers who hold fast to Christ by grace alone through faith alone. They are not constituted by outward ecclesial affiliation nor by outward ceremonies, rites, or works, but by faith in Christ. As such, the church is truly one in Christ even as it transcends the bounds of denominations, race, gender, age, language, and all the other things that humanly divide. It is that group who at all times and in all places confesses Christ as their savior without their merit or worthiness.

This powerful confession of Christ arose as an answer to both internal and external struggles. As a pastor, president, and dogmatician, Pieper constantly faced the double threat of Pietism and Rationalism which, on the one hand, sought to transform justification into sanctification and, on the other hand, sought to make Christianity one among many religions that essentially taught a system of morality. The end result of both of these threats, Pietism and Rationalism, was to move the center of Christianity away from Christ and toward the Christian. In both cases, works and morality replace Christ. For Pieper, however, Christ is always and must be the immovable center. All theology is Christology and, as such, everything rests on the work of God, his grace, his mercy, and his love.

While Pieper may be of parochial historical interest to some for his role in the LCMS, the theological questions with which he engaged are questions for all Christians of all times and places. The present work on the "nature" or "essence" of Christianity is no exception. Originally delivered as an address at a synod convention in 1902, "*Das Wesen des Christentums*" or "What is Christianity?" is a piece of both academic and pastoral concern. On the one hand, it directly addresses the academic milieu of the day, populated by the moralism and historical theology of Adolf von Harnack, whose influential lectures by the same title were taking hold of the Lutheran world. On the other hand, it also addresses the simple Christian in the pews, struggling under the weight of the law, in search of Christian identity, and in need of a quiet conscience. As such, Pieper addresses us today as both a pastor and a professor, a serious thinker and a shepherd of souls.

A note about translation

Older German texts relate emphasis in two primary ways. One that will be familiar to English speakers is the use of **bold** *which is called "Fettdruck". The second way to indicate emphasis is through the use of a spaced t y p e f o n t called "Sperrdruck" or "Sperrsatz". In this particular essay, Pieper makes very free use of the latter, which I have chosen to indicate through the use of italics. In one place, he uses the former, which is indicated with bold. These emphases, previously omitted in J. T. Mueller's translation, have been included to aid the reader in hearing Pieper's voice and stress. Where biblical citations occur, I have chosen to translate them directly from German into English instead of using a modern translation, to better match Pieper's usage. Likewise, where Luther is cited, in the majority of cases I have translated afresh instead of using the American Edition of* Luther's Works, *although parallel citations are given where available. Compared to the original translation by J. T. Mueller, a more literal approach to translation has been taken throughout, with a dedicated effort to* *maintaining the integrity of the address as a piece meant to be heard. The basis for this translation is the text of the "Fünfundzwanzigster Synodal-Bericht der Allgemeinen deutschen ev.-luth. Synode von Missouri, Ohio, und andern Staaten, versammelt als Zehnte Delegatensynode zu Milwaukee, Wis., im Jahre 1902", published by Concordia Publishing House in 1902. Thanks are owed to Dr. Larry Rast for providing the original text of the German and encouraging me in the work of translation. Thanks also to friends John Hoyum, Caleb Keith, and Adam Guthmiller, whose conversation was the genesis of this project.*

The Essence
of Christianity or
"What is Christianity?"

By Francis Pieper

Over the last two years, the nature of Christianity has been
debated by what seems like the whole of Christendom.
More precisely, the debate lies in *what Christianity really
is* and *how it is distinct* from all other religions. This
debate was brought to the fore by the lectures of the
Berlin Professor Adolf von Harnack on this subject.[1] What
Harnack said, and soon thereafter printed, does not, however, deserve the widespread attention that it has attracted.
The Berlin professor has merely repeated old, well-worn
assertions. In brief, Harnack's teaching is this: Christ is not

---

[1] PB: Adolf von Harnack delivered this series of lectures during the Winter
semester of 1899-1900 before a body of about 600 from all the faculties at Berlin.
They were recorded in shorthand, transcribed, lightly edited, and printed shortly
thereafter. They were met with overwhelming approval. As a testament to their
immediate popularity, the first English translation was completed in November
of that same year.

God, but a singularly wise and virtuous man.[2] Therefore, Christ neither kept the divine law *in man's stead* nor bore the penalty for the transgression of the law *in his stead*. Furthermore, Christianity is not constituted by *faith in Christ*, but rather in man's *own moral conduct*, which is motivated and guided by the unique personality of Christ. This teaching, as was said, is nothing new. The Unitarians and Rationalists of all times, which is to say those who deny the Holy Trinity and the so-called "reasonable theologians", have always taught this. But the fact remains that discussions about the nature of Christianity have popped up all across the globe because of Harnack's appearance.

And the result? The result is by no means agreement, even among those who call themselves Christian, and this should give us pause. We are faced with the fact that those who dub themselves "Christian" do not agree as to *what Christianity is*.

One could ask in bewilderment, *how?* Christianity has been in the world already for almost 2,000 years, indeed, almost 6,000 years if we consider the first proclamation of the promise of Christ—and people are still divided in Christendom over the nature of Christianity? People are still arguing about what Christianity really is?

---

[2] PB: The third lecture that Harnack gave in this series is especially exemplary of Pieper's point here: "It was to repentance and to inward conversion that he called them; to God, and therefore to the exertion of all their moral force; to truth and to the Spirit... By his powerful personality, and in union with friends of a like mind, he produced an immense impression." While Pieper is speaking very simply and perhaps could be construed as being uncharitable, Harnack does not confess the sonship of Christ in any orthodox sense, but rather places the central message of Christ in moral exertion and the divinity of Christ in his personality and participation in morality.

To this we say that, with regard to the nature of Christianity, *Christendom* is *totally in agreement*. In fact, all members of the Christian church agree that, through faith in Christ, the Savior of Sinners, regardless of their merit or works, they have forgiveness of sins and salvation. Through this faith and through nothing else are they indeed members of the Christian church. Whoever has this faith belongs to the Christian church; whoever does not have this faith does not belong to the Christian church. We can also include those souls who, though they outwardly belong to the Christian church under the papacy or among the sects, yet believe that they have the forgiveness of sins, not by their work or their own "morality", but on account of Christ. That is the one faith that the Apostle Paul ascribes to the Christian church when he wrote, "One Lord, one faith" (Eph 4:5). That is the "one spirit" that the Holy Spirit has created, and preserves, as we sing of the Holy Spirit: "Who the Christian Church his own creation,// Keeps in unity of spirit".[3] The faith and disposition of every Christian are expressed in the words of scripture: "The blood of Jesus Christ, the Son of God, makes us clean from all sin" (1 Jn 1:7) and "Now we hold that a man is justified without works of the law, through faith alone" (Rom 3:28). So also in the children's song: "Christ's crimson blood and righteousness// My glory are and spotless dress;// In this before my God I'll stand// And enter heav'n, my fatherland."[4]

---

[3] PB: Lutheran Service Book #954, stanza 3, "We all believe in one true God", by Martin Luther.

[4] PB: Evangelical Lutheran Hymnal #260, stanza 1, "Christ's crimson blood and righteousness", by Nicolaus Zinzendorf.

Dissenting opinions with regard to the nature of Christianity can only be found among those who *call* themselves Christians, but who are not Christians. Of those people who wish to approach God on the basis of their morality or their works, who set the nature of Christianity in morality, the scriptures say, "You have forfeit Christ, you who wish to become righteous through the law, and you have fallen from grace" (Gal 5:4) and "the ones who do the works of the law are under a curse" (Gal 3:10). These people also do not belong to the Christian church. Of the Christian church it cannot be said, "many heads, many minds". The Christian church is truly of one mind.[5] The Christian church is the congregation *of faith*, that is, the congregation that believes that they have forgiveness of sins for Christ's sake. *Luther* writes, "There is not more than one single Church, or people of God, on earth, which has the same faith, baptism, the same confession of God the Father and *Christ*, etc. and in such, peacefully hold and remain with one another. In this everyone must be found and to it everyone must belong who wishes to be saved and come to God; and outside of it no one will be saved."[6]

This, then, already answers the question of the nature of Christianity, both positively and negatively. It

---

[5] PB: Here and above, Pieper has in mind the confession of the Nicene Creed of the *una sancta* or the "one, holy, catholic, and apostolic church". In the Lutheran Confessions, the *una sancta ecclesia* is confessed in the Augsburg Confession, article VII, which states, "It is also taught that at all times there must be and remain *one holy, Christian church*. It is the assembly of all *believers* among whom the gospel is purely preached and the holy sacraments are administered according to the gospel" (emphasis added).

[6] St. L. Ed., XII. 898.

also already indicates how important it is to hold fast the nature of Christianity.

Nevertheless, it may be useful to venture somewhat further still into the topic. I will explain in detail by defending these two theses:

I. *The nature of Christianity is in faith in Christ, not in man's own moral conduct.*

II. *The Christian church must hold fast to the essence of Christianity, if she is to fulfill her service to the world.*

I. THE NATURE OF CHRISTIANITY

Let us, therefore, deal with the nature of Christianity in a little more detail. Concerning the "nature" of a thing, we take this to mean "what makes a thing what it is" or "that according to which a thing is what it is, whereby it is *distinguished* from other such things." So when we speak, for example, concerning the nature of man in contrast to the nature of animals, we find concerning the nature of man that, unlike animals, man has a rational soul.[7] This is also how we understand the nature of Christianity, namely, what makes Christianity Christianity and thereby what distinguishes Christianity from all other religions.

So what is that thing? What *in* or *about* a man makes him a Christian? It can't be wearing this or that piece of

---

[7] PB: This is a classical definition of man from Greek philosophy. Aristotle's *Metaphysics* notes that man is a naturally curious and perceptive creature and through his natural faculties is led to rationally contemplate the world. His *On the Soul* names reason and imagination, the creative link between the mind and the body, to be a unique attribute of man above all other animals. Aristotle's *Topics* explicitly defines the essence of man as being a rational animal. The *Moral Epistles* of Seneca likewise explicitly names man as a rational animal and reason being the thing proper to man in which he can glory.

clothing, as Luther reminds us. It also can't be that he has body and soul, and indeed a rational soul; nor that he is a man or a woman, young or old; nor also that he is educated or uneducated; nor that he is white, black, or yellow, etc. It also cannot be that he is an American or a German or an Englishman; nor still that he believes in a god or that he seeks to live an honorable life in accordance with the dictates of conscience and the law of the land. No, only *one* thing makes a man a Christian: faith in Christ; that man, while being a sinner, flees to Christ to find a gracious God and salvation.[8] This is what distinguishes Christianity from all other religions that exist in the world. All other religions are *religions of works*, that is, religions that direct men to secure the favor of God through their own goodness, their own effort, and their own works. On this point, *all* non-Christian and so-called Christian religions agree. It is only in the kinds of works they prescribe that the various religions are distinct. But Christianity is not a religion of works, but the religion of faith, the religion of faith in Christ. A *Christian* is a man who desires to enter heaven not through his own goodness and works, but through the righteousness and works of Christ.

Where does this come from? Whence is the nature of Christianity? Wherein lies the foundation for the nature of Christianity? What is the distinction between Christianity and paganism? It lies in this: that Christianity has a *Savior*;

---

[8] PB: Luther, in his "Disputation Concerning Man", defines a human being based off of St. Paul's words from Romans 3:28 "'We hold that a man is justified by faith apart from works.' briefly sums up the definition of a man, saying, 'Man is justified by faith.'" AE 34.139.

all other religions do not. The pagan religions have mere teachers, teachers who give moral precepts to men, who through their adherence must bring themselves to heaven. Christ, the incarnate Son of God, has taken a different approach. Christ has not preached a new law, but he has given himself in the place of man to be under the eternally binding law. This he obeyed in man's stead and paid the penalty for man's transgression in his stead through his death and the shedding of his blood. As the Scriptures testify concerning Christ, "When the time was fulfilled, God sent his Son, born from a woman and put under the law, in order that he might redeem those who were under the law" (Gal 4:4-5). And again: "See! The lamb of God, who bears the sin of the world" (Jn 1:29). "Surely, he bore our sickness and took upon himself our pain… He was wounded for our misery and crushed for our sin. The punishment was laid upon him so that we might have peace" (Is 53:4, 5). In sum, because the Son of God became man and as the God-man obeyed the law of God in man's stead and in his stead also paid the penalty for man's transgression of the law, thus becoming the *Savior* of all men, the nature of Christianity cannot consist in man's striving to keep God's law, but rather consists in *believing* in that man who has kept the law for him and for every sinner. Therefore Christianity is not a religion of works, but a religion of faith. The nature of Christianity subsists solely in faith in Christ. Luther used to say, "Someone is white because of his whiteness and black because of his blackness. Someone is a Christian because of Christ, which is to say that before God he flees to the works and suffering of Christ."

Of course, Christianity does teach morality and good works. As we will see later, true morality and good works can be found *only in Christianity*. But a Christian does not desire to be saved in part on account of his own goodness and works– not even halfway, a quarter of the way, or a thousandth of the way– but only on account of the righteousness and works of Christ. This nature of Christianity is already expressed in the memory verse every child knows: "God so loved the world, that he gave his only-begotten Son, that everyone *who believes in him* will not perish but have eternal life" (Jn 3:16). This nature of Christianity, which distinguishes it from all other religions, has also been aptly pointed out by the known linguist Max Mueller,[9] when he held a lecture for the bible society concerning the sacred text of Christianity, the Bible. Among other things, the renowned Orientalist said, "Over the last 40 years fulfilling my duties as a professor of Sanskrit at the University of Oxford, I have dedicated more time than any other person in the world to the study of the sacred texts of the East. And I would dare to say to this assembly that I have found the unifying motif of all these so-called sacred texts, the primary motif, the one refrain which prevails through all of them, is *salvation by works*. They all teach that salvation must be bought. Our own Bible–our sacred text from the East– is from beginning to end a protest against this teaching.

---

[9] PB: Max Mueller (1823-1900) was a professor of philology and Sanskrit at Oxford. Especially later in his career he was often attacked for his work studying and comparing ancient pagan religions to Christianity. Despite being called anti-Christian and even an atheist, he remained a Lutheran his whole life.

Good works are also certainly required in that sacred text of the East, but they are only the outpouring of a grateful heart–they are only a thanks offering, the fruit of our faith. They are never the ransom money of true disciples of Christ. Let us not close our eyes against that which is noble and true, but let us teach the Hindus, Buddhists, and Mohammedans that there is only one sacred text of the East, which is their only comfort in that grave hour when they must cross over into the unseen world alone."

Thus we have seen that—and why—*faith in Christ* is Christianity. Now let us consider the opposite point of view even more closely, namely, the opinion that Christianity consists in *man's own good works and righteousness.*

We reply that we certainly respect those people— though they are rare birds today—who earnestly endeavor to obey the commands of God in order to be saved. The Apostle Paul also testifies of the Jews who sought to establish their own righteousness "that they have zeal for God" (Rom 10:2). Such people are certainly more beloved to us than those coarse degenerates who live without shame according to their own passions. The righteousness of works, the *justitia operum*, has—as our confessions emphasize repeatedly—immense worth *for the state* and *life as a citizen.* We live a more peaceful life in a society of honorable men than among depraved people. And of course, God rewards those who are honorable with earthly goods. But it is completely wrong if someone were to try to make what is of worth in the state and in life as a citizen prevail also *before God* and thereby *be righteous and blessed before God.*[10] As we have heard, Paul says of the Jews who sought to establish their own righteousness that they have zeal for God, but he also adds "without understanding" (Rom 10:2). Their zeal is such that *they are without understanding* and *they are spiritually blind.* Therefore we say that whoever agrees with Professor Harnack that the nature of Christianity consists in man's own morality, such one is spiritually not right in the head, is blind, indeed stone-blind; he has no idea what the nature of Christianity is; he has even confused paganism and Christianity and is stuck in the religion of the *flesh.* The Scriptures state this explicitly.

The flesh expresses itself in relation to religion in a twofold manner. On the one hand, it says that there is no God, nor heaven or hell, all religion is folly, and let us eat, drink, [and be merry]. That is the *materialistic* flesh. On the other hand, there is the flesh that says there is a God and, in order to come to him, one must avoid sin and do the good. This is the *religious* flesh. But it is nevertheless *flesh.* If anyone desires to approach God on account of his own morality and works, that is the flesh, as the Scripture calls it. When the Galatians, who were seduced by the false teaching of the Jews, forsook the Gospel for the law when they desired to be righteous before God through their own works instead of on account of faith in Christ, the Apostle Paul says to them, "O you *foolish* Galatians, who

---

[10]   PB: Here Pieper is employing a helpful distinction that Luther often uses between the three forums of life: before God (*coram Deo*), before man (*coram hominibus*), and before oneself (*coram meipsum*). These three fundamental relations of life are often used in the discussion of one's righteousness and works and what purpose or use they serve.

has bewitched you, that you have not obeyed the truth?...
Having begun in the Spirit, do you now desire to be complete according to the flesh?" (Gal 3:1, 3). It is also called a *carnal* mindset and walking according to the *flesh* when someone desires to come to God through their own deeds. God's judgment here is different from the judgment of man. It impresses us or, to borrow a phrase from Luther, "it makes people's jaw drop" when someone really tries, or at least seems to be making an honest effort, to live an outwardly upright life according to the precepts of the law, with vigils, fasting, chastening oneself, and other extraordinary works, in order to earn heaven. We men are inclined to call all this "spiritual", but according to the Scriptures, this is the vain way of the flesh. Even if someone were to give all that he had to the poor, fast himself nearly to death, scourge himself bloody, even ripping the flesh off his body bit by bit, thinking that he could thereby purchase the grace of God, even after all that, it would still just be *flesh*. Concerning Galatians 3:3 ("Having begun in the Spirit, do you now desire to be complete according to the flesh?"), Luther writes, "By 'flesh' he does not mean sexual lust, animal passions, or the sensual apetite... 'Flesh' is the very righteousness and wisdom of the flesh and the judgment of reason, *which wants to be justified through the Law.*"[11] In sum, the desire to be righteous on account of one's own works is characteristic of blind paganism; desiring to be blessed without works, through faith in Christ, that is the characteristic of Christianity.

---

[11] St. L. Ed. IX. 288. (AE 26:216)

This is why Christianity is a *deep mystery, hidden* from natural man. Harnack claims that what John the Baptist and Jesus himself had taught, mankind *already* knew in essence. He says, "What is there that can have been 'new,' seeing that mankind existed so long before Jesus Christ and had seen so much in the way of intelligence and knowledge?"[12] But Harnack's opinion is based on the false assumption that Christ only taught *morality* or the *law of God. The law*, however, is nothing new to men. *Pagans* also know the law of God, as the Scriptures so often and explicitly testify. The pagans not only know that there is a God (Rom 1:19), but also "God's righteous decrees" (Rom 1:32). The works of the law are written on their hearts, their consciences bearing witness (Rom 2:15). When missionaries preach the law to pagans, they preach nothing new. The divine law written in the heart of fallen man has become somewhat obscured, but it has not thereby been completely erased. As such, we also find among the pagans, as Luther says, splendid summaries and surveys of the law, in which not only evil works, but also evil thoughts and desires are denounced as sin.[13] In brief, Christianity and the pagan religions have the *law* in common; though, in the divine word of revelation, Christianity has the divine law in its original and perfect purity. But one thing is *totally unknown* to the pagans. It is totally unknown to them that there is someone who has *kept* the law for them. It is totally

---

[12] PB: Adolf von Harnack. *What is Christianity?* 2nd Revised Edition. Translated by Thomas Saunders. New York: G. P. Putnam's Sons, 50.

[13] PB: Melanchthon in numerous writings and commencement addresses lauds the *Ethics* of Aristotle in particular, and Luther likewise can often be found praising Cicero's work on ethics.

unknown to them that God has sent his Son into the world in order to satisfy the law in the place of man, so that man is saved *without works*, through faith in Christ. Paul calls this Gospel of Christ "the secret, hidden wisdom of God . . . which none of the princes of this world have known." This Gospel of Christ he designates as something "that no eye has seen, nor ear heard, neither entered into the heart of man" (1 Cor 2:7-9). And this Gospel of Christ the Apostle Paul calls the *true essence* of all Christian doctrine, as he says in the same place, "I constrain myself among you to know nothing, but Christ alone, the crucified." The pagan world, which sits in darkness and in the shadow of death, sees the light only when the Gospel of Christ is preached to them, when the message is brought to them: "You are reconciled with God on account of Christ; grace is yours on account of Christ without your work; abundant grace is here for you. Believe this, that you have a gracious God."

That is the essence of Christianity.

II. The Christian Church and Her Service to the World

And the Christian church must hold fast to this if she is to fulfill the mission given to her in this world and do what God has put her in the world to guard and do.

Why is the Christian church in the world?

1.

Chiefly and above everything else, to save people. Through the state, people are externally kept in order; but through the church, people are led unto salvation. That is the mission of the church in the world. For anyone who still desires to be Christian, this is unquestionably the purpose of the Christian church.

But how does the church achieve her purpose? Solely and exclusively through the sermon of the *Gospel of Christ crucified*. The church must preach that God has made him to be sin who knew no sin, in order that we might become the righteousness of God (2 Cor 5:21). This Gospel of Christ is the power of God unto salvation for everyone who believes (Rom 1:16). On account of morality and works shall no flesh be justified before God (Rom 3:20). Conversely, everyone who walks in the works of the law is under a curse (Gal 3:10). Just as it is certain that whoever believes in Christ has a gracious God, however, it is also certain that those who instead thrust their own morality before God do not have a gracious God. What will happen if the church places the nature of Christianity, not in the Gospel of Christ, but in man's own morality; if she makes the virtues and works of man the foundation instead of the grace of God in Christ? *This* is what would happen: she would lead men into eternal damnation, not salvation. With this sermon of works, the church would be the *biggest fraud* in the whole world. There is a great deal of fraud in the world. In the selling and exchange of goods, things are constantly represented as other than they actually are, with the result that people are intentionally robbed of their earthly goods. But the greatest fraud in the world is a church that replaces the preaching of the Gospel of Christ crucified with human works as the ground of salvation. The Apostle Paul says concerning men's salvation that by works of the law no flesh shall be justified (Gal 2:16).

In this sense, the greatest deceiver of both the world and man is the *papacy*. The papacy seeks to lure people with the promise that it will safely lead men to salvation; indeed, it alleges to be the only church in which there is salvation. When people fall into the lap of the papal church on account of these promises and this alluring claim, they are instructed to trust in their own works and the works of the saints instead of Christ crucified, and as a consequence, as many as enter the papal church are led with a great multitude into hell. If people under the papacy are saved—and such people do exist—they are saved by rejecting the papistic teaching of works and by instead, with great sorrow over sin and fear of death, holding fast to Christ as their only redeemer. The papacy is the *largest fraudulent enterprise in the world* because it has cloaked its *teaching of works* in the appearance of churchliness. The Lodges also defraud man and the world by their religion of works.[14] That Christ crucified is the one through whom all men must come to God is

---

[14] PB: Pieper's attacks against the Lodges and Freemasonry historically have their roots in the General Council of the Evangelical Lutheran Church which was founded in 1867. The Council was formed as a reaction to the "american-ization" of the church represented by Samuel Schmucker. The chief concerns that were discussed have been dubbed the "four points" and include whether or not Lutherans could accept the chiliasm, non-Lutheran pulpit exchange, non-Lutheran communicants, and Lodge membership alongside congregational membership. In 1872 the General Council adopted the Akron-Galesburg rule penned by Charles Portfield Krauth, which took an exclusive approach and said in essence, "Lutheran pulpits for Lutheran pastors; Lutheran altars for Lutheran members." As such, within the General Council, being a member of a secret society, Lodge, or Freemason group was prohibited.

enormously annoying for them. They would rather attain a better afterlife on the basis of their own perfection. The *sectarian preachers* are also deceivers of humanity because they teach that Christianity consists in following the "Golden Rule", and they describe conversion simply as trying to lead a better life.[15] We would also be deceivers of humanity if we followed the Berlin professor and desired to establish the nature of Christianity as man's morality. We could lead no one to salvation if our teaching was such. All our preaching would be in vain. All our church offerings would be in vain. All our synodical conventions would be in vain. If the nature of Christianity consisted of our own morality instead of faith in the Gospel of Jesus Christ for the forgiveness of sins, if we must save ourselves through our own works, then I would make a motion that we immediately adjourn and go home.[16] We would be absolutely useless in the world; we wouldn't be able to lead a single person to salvation, for by works of the law shall no flesh be justified. I don't know what else we could do except pronounce death upon the whole world and ourselves.

We must remain disentangled with the old, yet ever new, error that the nature of Christianity rests in man's morality. No, no! Christianity subsists in faith in the *Gospel*, in faith in the forgiveness of sins, which Christ

---

[15] PB: Probably a reference to the revival preachers of Pieper's day who preached without a regular call to a congregation (sectarian) and who emphasized sincere conversion and good works (Golden Rule).

[16] PB: This paper was originally an address at the 1902 synodical convention in Milwaukee, WI. Here Pieper is referring to the Rules of Order that govern synod conventions and injecting some light humor into his address.

has gained for all men. By preaching this, we save people and fulfill the purpose of the Christian church.

2.

Furthermore, the Christian church ought to provide men with a *quiet conscience before God* and, therefore, the highest happiness that there is for men here on earth. In view of the Divine Service,[17] a man ought to be able to say in every circumstance of life—whether sickness, poverty, or even in the midst of death—that "I know I have a gracious God; God is no longer wrathful toward me, but rather God loves me as a father loves his child." When a church as such does not do this, it is no longer of any use in the world. Christ's testament rings out: "Peace I leave you; my peace I give you" (Jn 14:27). The church exists to execute this last will and testament of the Lord.

But how does this happen? How does the church alone provide this peace of conscience? How does the church alone instill in the hearts of men the confidence to say, "We have the forgiveness of sins and a gracious God"? Through the Gospel alone; through faith alone in Christ, the Savior of sinners. "Therefore, since we have been justified by faith, we have peace with God *through our Lord Jesus Christ*; through him, we have also obtained access through faith into this grace, in which we stand, and we rejoice in hope of the glory of God to come" (Rom 5:1-2).

---

[17] PB: In German, "*den Dienst der christlichen Kirche*". "*Dienst*" or "service" can take on the peculiar meaning of the church "service". In view of Pieper's previous emphasis on the "sermon" of Christ crucified, I've chosen to translate this as "divine service" to further highlight the mission of the church fulfilled in the activity of the church as such, gathered on Sunday morning for Word and Sacrament ministry.

The teaching of works, trust in one's own morality, never lets the conscience rest under the accusation
of the divine law. God's law is a formidable thing. It is
a *divine* thing. As it is *written* in the Scriptures and our
own hearts, God's law always condemns us and gives us
an evil conscience as long as it finds the slightest vestige
of sin in us. This verdict of God's law to damn cannot be
abrogated through man's thoughts or deeds, but only by
another divine judgment; which is to say, the law can only
be abrogated through the divine judgment of the Gospel,
whereby *God himself* for Christ's sake absolves sinners of
their sins. An evil conscience yields to only **one** treatment:
the *blood of Jesus Christ*, the Son of God, applied to the
heart by faith. Professor Harnack, however, believes that
he can quiet the conscience *without the blood of Jesus*.
He gives the counsel that a person ought to *imagine* that
God is his Father, following Christ's example. According
to Harnack, everyone ought to confidently lift his head
high and call God his Father, irrespective of the person
and work of Christ in the Gospel, which is to say, without
faith in Christ crucified. Harnack can *talk about* confidence and *invite* us to be confident as much as he wants.
To quote Luther, however, such confidence remains only
in the *words* and in the mouth and never enters the *heart*.
And even if the whole world were to hold hands and shout
for ten years, indeed, even a lifetime: "We do not believe
Christ's blood was shed for us! But God is gracious to us
nonetheless!" *they would still be condemned by their own
hearts and consciences* and go to their graves with an evil
conscience.

The truth is that God is known, apprehended, and experienced as *gracious*, as *Father* only *in Christ* and never *outside of Christ.* The Jews want to call God their Father without Christ. They refuse, just as Harnack refuses, to accord the person and work of Christ in the Gospel. But Christ rebukes them: "Since you do not believe that I am he"—namely, your savior and the one who erases sin—"thus you will die in your sins" (Jn 8:24). No creature can bring peace and quiet to a troubled conscience; this is not the work of *men*, but of *God*. God *the Holy Spirit* must write the verdict of pardon in the place of the verdict of damnation in the conscience. The Holy Spirit is a Spirit who *preaches Christ.* Because he preaches Christ in the heart, the Lamb of God who bears the sin of the world, he thus wipes away the divine verdict of judgment in the conscience, and in its place, he gives the verdict of pardon and therefore confidence to say, "I have a gracious God." The teachers of works, who say that the nature of Christianity consists in man's own morality, may from time to time *lull* the conscience to sleep, but they cannot grant it peace. They are not *heralds of peace* for humanity, but *harbingers of torment.* In his explanation of Isaiah 52:7, Luther names those teachers of works, like the Papists and Harnack, "sad night owls" who "frighten with their screeching." But of messengers who bring the good news of Christ crucified he says, "How beautiful are their feet; for they bear with them the most joyful tidings for stricken consciences, as all whose consciences were once in peril know full well."[18]

---

[18] AE 17:209-210 (St. L. Ed. VI, 611.)

Of Isaiah 40:2, he says, "The forgiveness of sins does not rest in the works of men, nor even that man learns and does the law, but *simply* in the gracious remission of sins. One must hold fast to this saying. For when the terrified conscience feels the law, namely, the judgment of the law, on account of sin and the judgment of God, we must not take refuge in our own deeds and works. *For sin cannot be overcome by our own works*...A higher power, a mightier force, is required to overcome sin. The distressed soul must therefore first be taught to cast away all hope in its own merits and thereafter to cling to the promise: 'Her iniquity is forgiven' (Is 40:2) and cast itself upon Christ, who, to redeem us from the curse of sin, was made a curse for us, who suffered and was crucified, in order that through his victory over sin we might live a righteous life of faith as dear children, reconciled to the Father through the blood of his Son and justified by faith in him. *That is our teaching, and we know that it is well able to comfort all troubled consciences.*"[19] To this teaching, we must hold fast and we must reject Harnack and all teachers of works if we desire to quiet the consciences of others.

3.

The Christian church must also lead people to the Divine Service with the result that *they abound in good works*. To use a modern expression, the Christian church should cultivate a "Christian morality". This is *also* a result of the redemption which was accomplished on account of Christ.

---

[19] AE 17:4-7 (St. L. Ed. VI, 473.)

St. Paul writes in Titus 2:14 of Christ, "he has given himself for us in order that he might rescue us from all unrighteousness and cleanse a people set apart for himself, *busy with good works.*" We should always remember that man's good works do not count toward salvation. Only the perfect work of Christ avails for salvation. However, the good works of the Christian are not to be disregarded. They are extremely valuable. They are even of more worth than the whole world. On the last day, the world and everything in it will be consumed in fire, but the good works of the Christian will not be destroyed but will follow them into eternity, being crowned by God with a glorious reward of grace. Good works are an eternal treasure that Christians should collect for themselves here on earth. It is among the duties of a Christian pastor to also take care that the members of the congregation are rich in good works.

But how are good works produced? Only through faith in the Gospel; only when salvation through faith in Christ crucified without works of the law is learned. Whoever places the nature of Christianity in man's morality, in the works of man, loses both salvation and good works. No one has ever done a single good work until he believed that he has a gracious God *on account of faith in Christ* without his works.

Why? If a work is to be *good*, it must be done to *God*, with the *love of God* in the heart of the doer. But man after the Fall can only love God when he knows, believes, and experiences that God has had mercy on him in Christ and that God has redeemed him from everlasting damnation and given him heaven. When the Apostle Paul admonishes

Christians to "Christian morals", he says in Romans 12:1, "I admonish you through the *mercy of God* that you offer your lives as living sacrifices, holy and pleasing to God." "Through the mercy of God"—that is, by reminding men of the fact that God did not spare his only Son, but has given him up for us all. The doing of good works is an art that is limited to a certain class of people, and it is only those who believe in Christ as their savior who alone can do good works. Luther says, "Above all things, Christ must be *ours* and we *his* before we do good works"[20] and, in another place, "You must already have heaven and be saved" (namely, through faith in Christ) "before you do good works. Works do not serve heaven, but quite the opposite; out of sheer grace, heaven does good works without seeking a reward."[21]

Christian morality, above all—indeed, firstly—pertains to a *heavenly ethos*, an ethos that despises the vain things of this world and seeks after those things which are above. One does not acquire this ethos through poking and prodding, nor through flattery, and neither through moral instruction, culture, or science, but only through being given the heaven obtained through Christ. But this happens first and only through the Gospel and faith in the same. Everyone who does not have his treasure in heaven through faith in Christ finds their delight somehow in the draff[22] of this world. Nothing else is possible.

---

[20] Erlangen Ed. 10.43

[21] Walch Ed. 12:183

[22] PB: "Draff" is the term for grain after it's been used in the process of brewing beer. In good German fashion, Pieper is comparing one's treasure in heaven by grace through faith to drinking good German beer and one's treasure on earth to consuming the spent grain after brewing.

Whoever robs the Christian church of this teaching—that we have a gracious God and salvation without our works, but through faith in Christ alone—also robs the church of good works. And yet, since the time of the Apostles, there have been many people who call themselves Christian who have argued that if "morality" and good works are to abound, one must push faith in Christ aside and emphasize the works of men. But this is proof that when man follows his own thoughts instead of God's word, he is ignorant, blind, stupid, wild, and crazed. They are so insane. They are like someone who desires *fruit*, but in order to fulfill his desire, he cuts down the *tree* that is bearing fruit. No, there is an unassailable order between faith in Christ and good works. In the first place stands faith in Christ, and in the second place stands good works. Whoever would put good works first, therefore, destroys good works. Good works must remain in the second place or they do not remain at all; that is, they do not even exist. Outside of faith in Christ, there is an external, civil, natural morality that has a certain value for life as a citizen, but not *Christian* morality, not good works, because outside of faith in Christ there is no Holy Spirit, no mind directed by God, and no love of God. One can *talk* about the love of God outside of Christ as also the pagans have done. The Papists, Unitarians, Lodges, and others do the same. But this talk remains mere talk. Love for God and the neighbor after the Fall are implanted only one way: through faith in Christ, the Savior of Sinners. Therefore, anyone with Harnack and all the other teachers of works who want to claim that the nature of Christianity consists in man's morality instead of faith in Christ, are *enemies and destroyers of every good work*. The Christian church must not associate with them.

4.

Finally, the Christian church must make men wise and understanding, so wise and understanding that they can clearly distinguish truth and falsehood in religious matters. Christ our Lord says to those who belong to the church, "You will know the truth" (Jn 8:32).

But when and how do men come by this spiritual understanding? St. Paul writes in 1 Corinthians 2:15, "The *spiritual person* judges all things, and will be judged by no one." Who is this "spiritual person"? According to the context of the passage, it is not the *pastor* or any other *gifted person* in the church, but rather every *Christian*, that is, every man who knows and accepts the Gospel of Christ in faith, who knows that he has a gracious God and salvation, not on account of his own works, but through faith in Christ crucified. This is what the Apostle Paul preaches above all else to the Corinthians, as he says in the same place, 1 Corinthians 2:2: "I determined to know nothing among you except Jesus Christ, the crucified." This good news of salvation through Christ crucified the Apostle calls "the heavenly, hidden wisdom of God", which the princes of this world did not know, but which God has revealed through the Holy Spirit in the Gospel concerning Christ. And whoever believes this wisdom, this Gospel of Christ, is spiritually *wise*, spiritually *understanding*.

Here, at this point, is the dividing line between wisdom and folly among men. Whoever knows that he will be saved by faith in Christ without works is spiritually wise. Yet whoever thinks that the nature of the Christian religion consists in man's own morality is still spiritually unwise; he is not only *partially*, but *completely* blind, even if he otherwise possesses all the knowledge in the world. Christ, the Savior of Sinners, who has reconciled the world, is the *only spiritual light* for man. Whoever has not received this light, that is, whoever does not trust in the work and suffering of Christ, but rather seeks to establish his own righteousness before God, dwells in thick darkness. He does not understand the Old Testament, for the content of the Old Testament is Christ, the Savior of Sinners, as Peter testifies in Acts 10:43: "To him" (namely, Christ), "all the prophets bear witness that through his name whoever believes in him will receive the forgiveness of sins." Neither does he understand the New Testament, because the content of the New Testament is also Christ, the Savior of Sinners, as St. Paul testifies in his New Testament sermon: "I determined to know nothing among you except Christ, the crucified" (1 Cor 2:2). To such a person, the whole Bible is entirely unintelligible, a book sealed with seven seals, even if he knows every word of the Bible by heart. For all his talk about Christ, Christian morality, love of God and the neighbor, etc., he doesn't understand a thing about Christianity. He may think that a whole dozen ways lead to heaven and that he can be, according to his circumstances, either a Turk, a Jew, a Buddhist, a Papist, a Unitarian, a Lodge member, or anything else. There's a saying, "At night, all cats are grey." Everyone who thinks that they can and must enter heaven through their own morality wanders about at night in the deep darkness, considering their own spiritual path the same as others. Therefore they maintain that all religions are essentially the same. However, as soon as the light of the Gospel of Christ, the Savior of Sinners, dawns on man, then all erring in spiritual matters ends. Then he knows that there aren't a dozen ways that lead to heaven, but only *one single* way: trust in Christ crucified. He clearly and steadfastly rejects all religions as false that want to make the works of men the basis of God's grace and salvation. He remains unbeguiled by the Turks, Jews, Buddhists, Papists, Unitarians, Lodge members, and all other false religions.

So, we have seen why it is so important in every circumstance and against every error to maintain that Christianity subsists in faith in Christ crucified. Only by this can we save people, give them the certainty of divine grace, make them abound in good works, and make them spiritually discerning. May God graciously keep us in the truth of the Gospel for Christ's sake.